Beating Par In The Merger Game

Beating Par In The Merger Game

Mergers & Acquisitions the Easy Way

C. Raymond Rogers
Susan K. Graaff

Illustrations by Adam Oren Hollandsworth
Cover Art by Jeri G. Epperson

Writer's Showcase
New York Lincoln Shanghai

Beating Par In The Merger Game
Mergers & Acquisitions the Easy Way

Writer's Showcase
an imprint of iUniverse, Inc.

For information address:
iUniverse
2021 Pine Lake Road, Suite 100
Lincoln, NE 68512
www.iuniverse.com

ISBN: 0-595-26331-3

Printed in the United States of America

For William C. (Bill) Case

Whose energy and excitement about the potential for wildly successful merger experiences was the inspiration for this book. Bill wakes up saying "I just love the smell of mergers in the morning!"

For these two Thinkers, who kept the spirit and intent of the work alive and vibrant.

Ashley Ford Wiersma
Dr. Steve Schepman

CONTENTS

BOOK ONE: THE COURSE

BOOK TWO: THE GAME

BOOK THREE: CLEATS, CLUBS, AND GOLF CARTS
Tools of the Trade

Preface

Our intention was to publish a book in straight-forward terms about the exciting world of M&A integration and the foundational concepts needed for the challenging task of uniting and blending multiple organizations into one successfully. It was not meant to be an exhaustive study or an academic exercise, but a practical description of actions executives can take as they lead their organizations through this significant event. We intentionally have not added unnecessary filler, preferring to say it as simply and briefly as possible while maintaining the integrity of the process.

Knowing what to do is one thing;

Doing it is another.

Our hope is to leave you with an optimism that you <u>can</u> *Beat Par* in your next merger.

We would be happy to discuss any of the concepts, processes, or tools in this book in greater detail.

C. Raymond (Ray) Rogers
craymon_1@email.msn.com

Susan K. Graaff
susan@mergercoach.com

BOOK ONE
THE COURSE

BOOK ONE
THE COURSE

Chapter One
Introduction

Chapter One

Mergers and acquisitions are anything but " business as usual". Executives report that even though they may have been involved in mergers in the past, nothing had prepared them for the range and depth of issues needing resolution as a top decision-maker. The primary audience for this book is a chief executive contemplating a merger; the senior executives who are responsible for integrating the companies; or the project manager whose career will either rise or fall depending on how well the merger works. For purposes of simplicity and efficiency, we will refer to "mergers" to describe that group of business combinations that come under the heading of either mergers or acquisitions, without calling out when it is one or the other specifically.

Executives readily agree the probability of achieving the synergies identified in the deal-making stage would go up dramatically if the integration could be accomplished in a shorter period of time to protect sales revenue and production levels. They are often astounded to hear that two companies can put together an integration plan in ninety days that will guide the new company's actions for the next product cycle as well as the next two years.

The foundational processes and tools in this book have proven time and again to be the formula for achieving that ninety day speed to integration. These *processes and tools* are based on the following *three* premises that lead to a very powerful *formula for success* in merger and acquisition integrations:

Premise One:

MERGER DYNAMICS ARE PREDICTABLE. Once the merger is agreed to and the leadership begins the integration process, predictable business and organizational issues surface. That predictability can be leveraged and planned around to ensure the right energy and resources are focused on the right issues at the right time

---

Premise Two:

PEOPLES ACTIONS AND REACTIONS TO CHANGE ARE PREDICTABLE. Each level in the organization reacts predictably during significant changes such as a merger. The points at which these reactions will kick in during the integration process are also predictable. Actively seeking approaches that capitalize on the reactions of each level will pay off handsomely by turning those reactions into assets rather than liabilities

---

Premise Three:

SPEED IS YOUR FRIEND. The more time that elapses between announcement of a change and involvement of people in the change, the higher the risk of a negative reaction. That speed to change can be actively controlled by disciplined processes and consistency of determination

---

Integration Success Formula

Recognize the value of the Three Premises and utilize them correctly at specific points in the integration process
to give you

Direction
+
Discipline
+
DamnfastDelivery

The Ninety Day Payoff

What will you have at the end of a 90 day integration planning period that will make the effort worthwhile?

- Desired synergies defined for both cost and revenue in the short and long term

- Efficiencies that define the deal and translate into cost savings and/or revenue increases

- An accurate description of the perceived value of the optimum state with numbers attached for all resources

- Cultural attributes defined for what is valued in behaviors; what is measured; desired way of operating; acceptable performance

- Retention controlled, keeping the right talent in the right place at the right time at the right cost

- Go-forward operational strategy ready for deployment

- Organization focused on deliverables and tactics to achieve the business vision

- Visibility of value and identity established in the right markets, reinforcing customer focus

- Functional interfaces outlined and core systems designed

We have chosen the game of golf as the continuing analogy throughout this book because executives in a merger are much like professional golfers. They know their game and are very good at playing their game. They know their company and are very good at playing their game in their company. When a merger occurs the executive's capabilities do not change, the course does. In the game of golf, different courses require golfers to use their skills and tools differently. Each merger, likewise, requires executives to use their skills and capabilities differently.

Merger coaches know mergers and acquisitions like a professional caddy knows the courses his golf pro is going to play. We have enjoyed extensive experience working closely with executives as they apply their unique knowledge, skills, and abilities to the job of envisioning and creating a new company out of former competitors. We have a proven record of helping executives not only meet, but exceed, the synergies projected at the inception of the deal. Our objectives were to make sure the executive could "beat par" in the merger game by estimating the distance accurately, predicting the lay of the fairway correctly to avoid the traps and hazards, hitting a clean shot with the right club, and holding steady at the pin for the full eighteen holes.

A successful merger during the early phases is controlled chaos. The end result of well-managed, controlled chaos is a merger that works because there is a comprehensive plan and a process that has the commitment of those key players that will be responsible for making it all work once it hits day to day operations.

This book will discuss the methods and processes we have used successfully in diverse organizations over the past decade. It describes what needs to occur to achieve a successful integration, when specific actions need to occur, and field-tested tools to accomplish the actions in the most efficient and effective way possible.

This book is laid out in three parts:

Book One—The Course, introduces general facts about the merger environment and summarizes key points of both the integration process and the tools that optimize its implementation.

Book Two—The Game, discusses the processes, timing and resource requirements of the integration in detail, illustrating the Direction + Discipline + DamnfastDelivery formula. It expands on the what, why and how of each action required during the 90 day integration process, aided by analogies and dialogue that illustrate how executives tend to react to the intensity and complexity of a merger. At the end of each of these three chapters, the process chapters, are key points to watch for as you move through integration titled *Watch The Traps*.

Book Three—Cleats, Clubs and Golf Carts, provides specific examples of tools that support each step of the process along with an explanation of when and why they are used.

BOOK ONE
THE COURSE

Chapter Two

"Taking Seven on a Par Five"

The merger and acquisition playing field

Chapter Two

Taking Seven on a Par Five
The Merger and Acquisition Playing Field

In any given year 9000 mergers occur. Estimates vary but the common number used to project the failure rate of these mergers is 83%. Using this estimate, over 7000 of those 9000 deals won't achieve the synergies projected. A pretty sad statistic when you consider the talent and capabilities of the people involved in crafting mergers, and the scores of books that have been written on the art of the deal.

An examination of scores on the PGA tour in any given year can provide some insights into the difference between success or failure. The average score separating the top money winners and those going back to qualifying school was less than three strokes per 18 holes. In a highly competitive environment a very small difference in performance can make a very big difference in who wins and who loses.

In mergers, being part of the 17% that succeed likewise turns on attention to a precious few imperatives. The reasons businesses merge vary widely, but the bottom-line objective is essentially the same, get more for your investment than you had before.

Mergers are consummated based on economic projections, often referred to as synergies, that use mathematical formulas and assumptions about leveraging that should occur as a result of the merger. The difficulty in leveraging the full potential of the combined companies is often not accurately anticipated. Cost reductions requiring consolidation of physical resources often underestimate how long it will take. Product rationalizations are harder to achieve than it would appear on paper. Market share does not always materialize as customers choose other suppliers.

Mathematical formulas are fundamental to the business game and when combined with "what if" scenarios can help executives gauge possibilities and risks. What they don't provide is insight into the intensity and rigor demanded in order to complete the actual integration of the companies into a healthy, vibrant, profitable, and competitive market force.

During the hunt for a deal, and the due diligence prior to finalization, the financial and legal aspects of a deal make clear technical distinctions between a merger and an acquisition. Once the deal is done, the question is not what to call it technically, but how you as the key executive will characterize the combination for planning and resourcing purposes. If you are looking at identifying and using the best practices of your strategy, business structure, systems, and skills—-then you are talking about the process of *integration*, which will require change in every part of the organization. If you are, instead, considering simply folding one company into another and will be making only minor modifications to the acquiring company's existing strategies, structures, systems and skills, you are talking about the process of *assimilation*. Assimilation requires a much less intensive resource effort than does integration, but does not necessarily engender any less resistance to the changes required. Each merger is different. Each merger has its own distinct characteristics and purposes. Understanding with clarity the merger you are facing will significantly speed up your ability to draw the right conclusions, make the right decisions, implement the right plans, and extract the right synergies. Whether you call it a merger or an acquisition is not terribly important. That you understand whether you intend to integrate or assimilate is terribly important.

While the top team undoubtedly invested a great deal of time and energy in making the deal, there will be a strong tendency to relax once the deal is signed. The job of integrating the companies is often delegated to the next level down or to a merger integration manager. What is overlooked or forgotten is that especially in times of uncertainty top leadership strength, clarity, and presence is more critical than ever.

BOOK ONE
THE COURSE

Chapter Three
"Hitting the Sweet Spot"

Executive Summary:
Key Facts. Key Tips. Key Tools

Chapter Three

Hitting the Sweet Spot

The Executive Summary of a Highly Successful Process For Merger and Acquisition Integrations

Professional golfers have a pre-shot routine they use before every shot regardless of the circumstances or situations they are facing. The discipline of doing the same thing, the same way before every shot helps them focus on the right things at the right time. Professional golfers also emphasize that to shoot a good score you think only about the shot that you are about to hit, not the shot you just hit or the tough shot you are going to have to hit two holes from now. You visualize executing that one shot exactly the way you want to hit the shot. The discipline of using a pre-shot routine and focusing only on the shot you are about to hit will improve the score you shoot for the total round.

In golf the sequence is first the right grip, second the proper setup to address the ball, and third a controlled swing. Grip, set up, swing. In mergers it follows the same: strategy first (get the grip right), structure second (set up for the future), and swing third (systems and methods that make the strategy and structure work). Strategy, structure, systems. Leaders must discipline themselves to follow the predetermined sequence and at each step focus on that specific activity.

Shortcutting the process just doesn't work. In golf shortcutting the sequence leads to missed shots and higher scores. You lose strokes to the better-disciplined players and increase your odds of losing. In mergers, shortcutting the sequence leads to missed opportunities and lower synergies, increasing your odds of losing.

The project structure that makes the process run, configured like the one below, ensures that decision-making for the critical integration planning is clear, the best resources are enlisted and engaged in best-practice thinking, and there is a disciplined method to deploy the sequenced process.

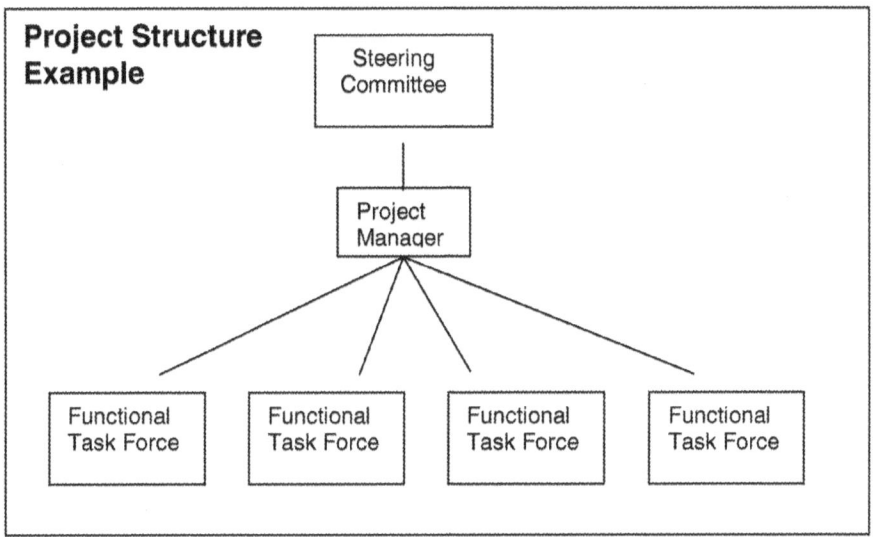

In mergers you are playing two events at the same time, running your business to make the "now" numbers and integrating your two businesses to achieve future numbers.

The advantage of a 90-day framework for the merger integration effort is that it puts a finite timeframe on the extraordinary effort that will be required. What has been amazing is the energy created by the double effort required. Keeping the pressure on getting results makes people focus on the essentials—keeping the quality, cost, and delivery requirements of the customer uppermost. When the essentials push to the front, unproductive side issues are delayed or eliminated.

The "event" of a merger being announced creates the defining moment for a leader to step-up and become the hero the organization so desperately wants in times of high uncertainty or confusion. At first the CEO may be a little apprehensive about the best approach in announcing the change and enlisting support, but the event itself will create the necessary rallying point and the need for the organization to focus on one point, the leader, becomes obvious.

It Isn't An Either-Or Question

Focus on Customers
Make it everyone's job to pour on the attention. Keep the customer involved in what is happening. Reassure them of your loyalty. Make them part of discovering potential in the integration solutions. Build them up.

Focus on Productivity
Keep sales and operations focused on the business. Provide information and training on what synergies are (both revenue and cost), where they come from, and how to get all of them. Encourage bold acts. Recognize courage.

Focus on Operations
Cut out the fat but not the muscle! Recognize the capabilities that work for the new organization and the ones that need retooling. Look at capacities with a critical, but informed, eye.

Focus on Bench Strength
Know where you are getting the most bang for the buck. Keep the first string in the starting lineup by getting the best people involved in the action. Know where it will hurt to lose and where it won't.

Focus on Speed
Keep up the pace. Don't look back. Keep the organization involved with aggressive forward movement on all fronts.

The top executive's job is to keep the senior team focused on both the business essentials and the merger integration process. It will mean double effort but it is for a finite timeframe and carries a big payoff.

Extraordinary events take extraordinary effort. The professional golfer who is required to play 36 holes of golf in one day because of a rain delay will tell you that it is difficult. The winner of the event will be the pro that keeps his focus on his task.

It is the senior team's job to keep the merger integration planning teams working within the project structure and focused on the sequenced integration process for ninety days, making sure it doesn't get cut short. To complete all of the moving parts of the process in the timeframe suggested—-ninety days or less—-you want to get as much accurate information as you can as quickly as possible in order to make good decisions. Input and involvement of as many people in your organization as possible is a key way of getting that information. The creation of a critical mass of key players who own the integration process because they played critical roles in shaping the new company is an added benefit.

In the midst of all the needed involvement, it is important to remember that successful mergers do not get implemented by either the extreme of autocratic decree or the extreme of full consensus. Running an integration is no different than running a strong business. They both require that the chief executive retain final decision power on all substantial issues. It is a balancing act. The savvy executive will use the process and the project structure to help ensure this balance is achieved without burning everyone out.

Executives play three critical roles during that first ninety days of a merger integration:

Communicator
Coach
Cheerleader

Communicator: As the communicator, major briefings each week to the organization will increase your accessibility and visibility during the uncertain times. People need the reassurance of your presence. They need to feel that you are in this with them. These briefings can take many forms, formal and informal, face-to-face, or through technology.

Coach: As the coach it is important not to sugar-coat reality, but rather to put the new reality into perspective. Recognize the power of your position and call on others to help you get things going. Now is the time to empower others through your direct involvement and by putting your personal stamp on what is about to happen.

Cheerleader: As the cheerleader, encourage people to see the potential benefits to the organization and to themselves of joining together. Recognize the efforts being made and every success, large and small. Watch carefully for any slumps and pump them up. Focus on the positive very publicly. Now is not the time to settle things down but to capitalize on the energy a significant change prompts. Remind people this is a short term focus, no more than ninety days

Grip fits hand,
Angle fits height,
Shaft fits swing,
Trophy fits mantel.

For the remainder of Chapter Three, the Integration Success Formula: *Direction + Discipline + DamnfastDelivery,* is arranged in the order in which it will come into play during the integration process. The key points have been synthesized into a high level Executive Summary for each one.

BOOK ONE
THE COURSE

Chapter Three
"Hitting the Sweet Spot"

Executive Summary:
DIRECTION

Course: Merion Golf Club (East)
Location: Ardmore, Pennsylvania
Architect: Hugh Wilson

Golfer: Bobby Jones
Bio Snapshot: Born in Atlanta, Georgia he is remembered as the 'epitome of golfing talent', and in the minds of many golfers was challenged only by Jack Nicklaus as the greatest golfer in history of the game. Bobby became a junior club champion at age nine; played his first U.S. Amateur tourney at age 14 at Merion Golf Club; won his first major, the U.S. Open, in 1923; and retired in 1930 at age 28 as the only golfer to win all Majors in a single year. In all, Bobby won 13 national championships in 8 years. He was a chain smoker, shied away from interaction with a curious, passionate gallery, and sometimes couldn't even eat during competitions. Bobby only practiced three months out of the year, spending the remaining time obtaining degrees in Law, English Literature, and Mechanical Engineering—all from different universities.

The Story: Bobby Jones made an appearance at Merion as a 14 year-old at the 1916 U.S. Amateur. Unfortunately, he was dispatched in the quarterfinals. Eight years later, he won his first U.S. Amateur title at Merion. Jones made a hero's journey to the club in 1930 to earn his fifth U.S. Amateur trophy and complete the fourth leg of his historic Grand Slam.

The Secret: The club has a storied championship tradition, and Pete Dye, one of the contributing course architects, put his finger on the reason: "Merion is not great because history was made there. History was made there because Merion is great. Chief architect Hugh Wilson's intent was not to duplicate other famous courses at Merion. Rather, he attempted to build a parkland course full of subtlety and nuance by fitting the holes to the land. What he came up with is the finest compact layout ever devised!"

When the plan fits the landscape, success is born.

DIRECTION

Scans, Strategies, and Product Roadmaps

Executive Summary

DIRECTION

Scans, Strategies, and Product Roadmaps

Setting Your Course Direction

The integration strategy process has three results.

o   A clear, concise description of the new company's scope and direction over the next 18 to 24 months

o   An understanding of the interdependence needed among the senior executives to achieve success

o   An evaluation of the capabilities of the senior executives by each other and the C.E.O.

Prior to the merger each company had a strategy for penetrating its chosen market. The strategies may have been highly intuitive or highly formalized. The interpretation of these strategic issues affected the discussions that occurred while crafting the deal and had implications on the outcome of decisions for how the companies should become one, and for what they should achieve by this combination.

Requiring the senior executives of the merged companies to jointly develop a visible integration strategy for the new company is an important opening move and accomplishes the following:

- The assumptions, viewpoints, feelings and attitudes of the management of each company becomes visible and can then be discussed and constructively aligned
- Both what is known and what is not known about the products, markets and capabilities of each company is visible and can be assessed and addressed
- Critical working relationships begin to form and commitment to the direction the new company needs to undertake starts to occur

Focusing on the integration strategy is critical at the beginning of a merger because it can bring strong alignment to diverse staffs. The top executive should convey to the staffs an expectation for that new alignment to be manifested in observable action when they face the organization. There is a need for the leadership to be of one mind, one voice, and one heart quickly. During chaotic times people require leaders who provide clarity, solidarity, and a vision they can respond to, not ones who add confusion and uncertainty to an already ambiguous situation.

The participants in integration strategy sessions are the top four or five executives from each company. These senior executives must provide a concise picture of the scope and direction of the merged company over the next two years. That will require undivided attention for specific and defined periods of time over the first weeks following announcement of the deal. This strategic team would expect to meet twice. A first session of two to three days to break the ice, get the feel of the group, introduce the preliminary questioning around the competitive position of the companies, begin to surface and compare expectations and cultures, and to draft a preliminary strategic document that requires further research for completion. A second session of three days, occurring within two weeks of the first one, to get down to brass tacks based on the data gathered in the intervening weeks about the product, market, and service combinations that will make sense over a transition period of the next several product cycles.

Because the integration strategy forms the foundation for structure and placement decisions that still need to be made within a fast ninety day integration window, it should be completed within thirty days of the announcement that the deal closed.

One Mind, One Heart, One Voice

Requiring the senior executives of the merged companies to jointly develop a visible integration strategy for the new company brings strong alignment to diverse staffs. There is a need for the leaders to demonstrate one mind, one voice, and one heart quickly.

Converting Direction Into Action

If the first step to success is a clear, specific direction, right on its heels is articulation of that direction to the organization. The message top executives should paint is the compelling picture of what is currently happening and what will be happening over the next ninety days. People want information and facts. The rumor mill will be running at full speed so you will need to use every communication tool at your disposal to tell and retell the what, how, why and when story. The benefits of having agreed up front on a clear, logical project process and plan with definite timelines that can be communicated, cannot be overstated as one of the most powerful ways to counteract those rumors. The senior executives are the perfect conduits for this information because they are the ones in possession of the best knowledge of what is happening and why.

To help executives understand why particular types of communication are most effective at particular times in the integration, there is an excellent model available that describes how people tend to confront significant change in their lives and it applies perfectly to the merger event. It is a well-researched and long running model that indicates people do react predictably to change and that there are several fairly simple things that can be done to help them move along and through that change.

It is called a Change Curve and what it says, in essence, is that all people will move along the curve at varying speeds and with varying intensity depending on their own particular personality. But they will move along that curve. It isn't a lockstep forward movement. Some days a crisis occurs and people move backward and have to begin the process again. The encouraging part of the change curve is that, given the right kind of inputs, people can and will move consistently through the curve until they arrive at the constructive, contributing posture called Search for Solutions that is most helpful and healthy to them and to the organization at large.

It looks like this:

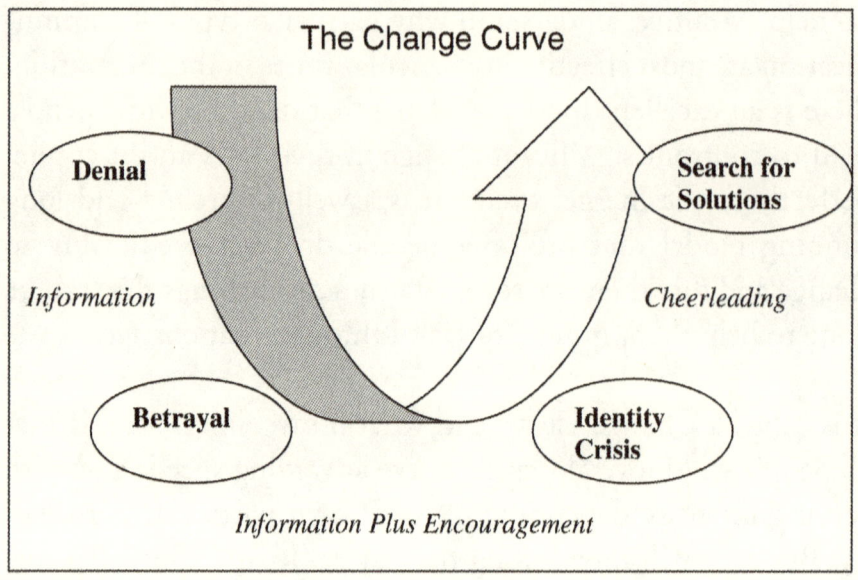

During the Betrayal and Denial Stages, people need information. Lots and lots of it. As they move along the curve into the
Identity Crisis Stage, they still need straightforward facts, but
now those facts need to be coupled with statements of understanding and encouragement. When they begin to move into
the Search for Solutions Stage you can begin cheerleading.
They are now ready for the vision and for visionary language.

Returning to your roles as Coach, Communicator, and
Cheerleader during change, examples of the types of information that can be provided to move people along the curve more
quickly are illustrated below:

Talk Your Head Off

Information
What are the key messages to *communicate*?

- There is a plan
- There are proven processes
- There is a set time limit for it to be done
- Their help is needed
- There will be a consistent and constant exchange of information among and to all parts of the organization
- It is a team effort

Information Plus Encouragement
What are the key pieces of advice to *coach* around?

- Things will change and that is healthy
- This is the time to step up and be noticed
- Mistakes will be made so go ahead and ask forgiveness now
- There is a need to go fast

Cheerleading
What are the key ideas to *cheerlead* about?
- Successful accomplishment of each step of the process
- The unique opportunity to make a difference individually in creating a new organization

By applying speed and discipline you can shorten the duration of the effects of the curve, and by applying involvement, education, and communication you can lessen the severity of the drop in focus and productivity during the change. Shorter duration and less drop equals savings in time, money, effort, stress, productivity, and quality.

Knowing the stages in the change curve and how to impact people and groups as they move along that curve, you can begin to positively control the energy of the organization You can provide a measure of predictability in the human reactions you are seeing in the organization, and you can get in front of it to effect it in constructive ways.

BOOK ONE
THE COURSE

Chapter Three
"Hitting the Sweet Spot""

Executive Summary:
DISCIPLINE

Course: Mid-Ocean Club
Location: Tucker's Town, Bermuda
Architect: Charles Blair MacDonald

"Golfer": Babe Ruth
Bio Snapshot: Born George Herman Ruth on February 6, 1895, in Baltimore, MD; Babe debuted as a pitcher for the Boston Red Sox, winning 89 games over six seasons before his trade to the Yankees for $125,000 in 1920. He was converted to the outfield because of his prodigious throwing power, and launched an amazing home run career, belting 60 in 1927 for a 714 lifetime total. Babe was elected to Major League Baseball's Hall of Fame in 1936 with 215 votes of 226 cast, or 95.13%. He was the first great slugger in the sport and the most celebrated athlete of his time.

The Story: Mid-Ocean's fifth hole is a real challenge with the strength and changing direction of the wind to consider. The temptation to bite off a good-sized chunk of the hazard by going directly over the lake is great, but the trip is longer that it appears. Robert Trent Jones, Jr., described the direct route over the lake from the elevated tee as "one of the most truly heroic tee shots ever conceived". Golfers must figure on a carry of at least 225 yards to the far shore in line with the tee box, more if the golfer is prone to hook. If attained, the far left edge of the fairway offers a shorter approach and a superior angle to the green. Perhaps this was Babe Ruth's line of reasoning when he made Mid-Ocean's fifth hole infamous in the 1930s. The Great Bambino reportedly swatted eleven straight tee shots into the drink trying for that far left edge before calling it quits!

The Secret: On Mid-Ocean's fifth hole, judging the shot angle correctly and understanding wind direction is only half the battle in finding the safety of the fairway on the other side. Golfers that clear the lake are rewarded with a two-tiered, banana-shaped green almost as challenging as the tee shot itself.

Perseverance is its' own reward.

DISCIPLINE

Structures, Systems, and Decision-Making

Executive Summary

DISCIPLINE

The Business and Organization Structures

Provide the Organizational Context

Every organization needs a hierarchy in place to assure that decisions are aligned from strategic, tactical and operational perspectives.

Business models have varying degrees of decision-making and autonomy which will drive time, effort, and resource utilization. For example: a business unit allows for more independent decision-making closer to the customer, while a matrix organization requires higher collaboration to reach a decision, and a traditional structure pushes cross-functional decisions upward through the organization.

At the business model stage of the planning process, the only position placements that should be agreed and announced are the Chairperson and the CEO. Organization structures aren't discussed and names don't begin appearing in boxes on an organization chart until after the business model has been completed.

Just as each organization coming into the merger had its own strategy, it also had a business model and organization structure in place that assured decisions got made and actions were taken. When a merger occurs the differences between the two structures must be resolved. Selecting the best business model for the combined companies is guaranteed to have many traps. The careers of some highly successful people may be on the line. Losing or gaining power is at stake. Protecting the status quo feels, and sometimes is, safer. Fortunately, the presence of a clear strategic direction for the new company will set a solid foundation and boundaries for the business model discussions.

It is critical to stress, once again, that the only names identified at this point are the Chairman and the CEO. The senior executives will have turf protection issues that may keep them from seeing the best business model solutions. The senior executives can be reassured they will have a role in the future organization, but they will not be tempted to promise appointments to their people if they are not yet assigned to a specific area and position. There will be tremendous pressure from the senior executives and from others in the organization to fill in the boxes in the organization chart too quickly. If you put names in boxes now, you will build what you already have instead of what you need. Business structure options will become limited.

Within thirty days after completion of the integration strategy work, a task force composed of senior executives from each company would be expected to spend several multiple-day sessions, using a rigorous analytic process, to select the best business model to deploy the integration strategy.

Immediately upon completion of the business model, that same task force must shift gears slightly and begin the task of populating the physical organization chart that will operate the organization on a day-to-day basis. Each name placed in a box on the organization chart must fulfill clear and specific pre-determined requirements for that position. It is at precisely this point in the process that emotion is likely to boil over. There is territory at stake now and empires to build. There is a history among the newly appointed executives and people they are loyal to. The heated discussions that take place here are invaluable, managed constructively, in visualizing and then placing the optimum capability in the optimum spot to ensure the strategy is accomplished.

BOOK ONE
THE COURSE

Chapter Three
"Hitting the Sweet Spot"

Executive Summary:
DAMNFASTDELIVERY

Hole: Ballybunion Golf Club (Old)
Location: Ballybunion, County Kerry, Ireland
Architect: Patrick Murphy, Tom Simpson, Molly Gourlay

Golfer: Tom Watson
Bio Snapshot: Born Thomas Sturges Watson on September 4, 1949, in Kansas City, MO, he majored in psychology at Stanford University before turning pro in 1971. In his career he won 34 PGA Tour victories, 9 International victories, and after joining the Senior Tour in 1999, won 2 Senior PGA Tour victories. In 1999 Tom was made an honorary member of the Royal & Ancient Golf Club of St. Andrews, joining fellow Americans Arnold Palmer, Jack Nicklaus, former President George Bush, and the late Gene Sarazen.

The Story: Herbert Warren Wind, the dean of American golf writers, put Ballybunion on the map by describing the links in 1971 as "nothing less than the finest seaside course I have ever seen." But not until Tom Watson arrived in 1981 to tackle the links and later sing its praises did pilgrims wake up to the idea that Ballybunion was well worth a detour, given that pars here are as rare as the fabled four leaf clovers.

> <u>The Secret</u>: "To succeed at the eleventh, it is not enough to advance your ball meekly down the fairway. No, the hole must be played with abandon, as the Irish do, holding nothing back. 'Have a lash at it, lad—and hope for the best'".—Brian McCallen
>
> 'Have a lash at it lad—and hope for the best'

DAMNFASTDELIVERY

Leadership, Leverage, and Energy Points

Executive Summary

In golf improving your score means doing something different in the way you think about, as well as execute, your grip, your setup, and your swing. As you persevere through using any change in your technique, the awkwardness disappears, skill improves, and satisfaction with the change increases because your results improve . Soon you can't believe you didn't always do things the new way. The same process will occur in a merger.

Strategic direction and the business model decisions generally result in requirements for new behaviors. New ways of behaving require an initial exertion over and above the normal in order to get them to stick, to become habit, to become second nature. In the beginning any new skill feels uncomfortable and awkward.

Many people in the organization have a major stake in pushing a "business as usual" stance to protect their resources, projects, ambitions, and job security. Many mergers are still struggling with overcapacity, redundancy and slow, antiquated methods years after the completion of a merger because of a "business as usual" mentality and unaddressed resistance to change caused by this bias.

Merger deals include, at the very least, implicit expectations that changes in operational actions will be needed. Eliminating over-capacity, removing redundancy, and streamlining methods were undoubtedly discussed as the types of issues that would need resolution when the two entities become one. These are emotionally charged issues.

The best way to channel emotions into constructive paths is to provide a logical process for problem solving and solution generation. A process will provide the form needed to increase the involvement of a broad spectrum of the organization and bring together the best thinking, focusing the energy on key business issues. It provides a common language and framework that will improve the timeliness and accuracy of decisions, and keep things on schedule. An additional benefit is a much higher retention rate of key employees as they get excited about the opportunity to be valued and deeply involved in shaping their destiny.

Using tools and approaches such as those outlined in detail in Chapters Seven, Eight, and Nine, will allow managers and individual contributors to see legitimate ways to provide positive input into the integration. It will identify ways they can contribute meaningfully to the potential of the new company. These contributors are not super-heroes. They are ordinary people with a desire to do extraordinary work for the organization's long-term health. You already have a bead on some of them because you have worked with them....but ask around....chances are extremely good there are a lot of other individual contributors in your organization who will fit this bill nicely, and who are just waiting to be given the chance. At the same time, be selective and picky about who you select to serve on the integration task forces. They are the ones who are planning your new organization and will be the ones who ensure you get the right results quickly.

A powerful and overlooked benefit of a disciplined process is the ability for the top executive to watch closely how potential managers in the organization work under stress and in critical situations. What a great lab. You can, in a controlled environment with low risk, take a look at potential resources that may just have the "right stuff" for your new organization. *Watch for it.* There are always some pleasant surprises.

THE GAME

BOOK TWO
THE GAME

Chapter Four
GRIP—<u>Direction</u>

*Scans, strategies, and product
roadmaps*

Hole: Tournament Players Club at Sawgrass Stadium
Location: Ponte Vedra Beach, FL
Architect: Pete Dye

Golfer: David Duval
Bio Snapshot: Born Robert David Duval on November 9, 1971, in Jacksonville, FL. His father, Bob, is a senior PGA player and David caddied for his dad at his dad's first Senior Tour event. David ranked 69th in money leaders on the 1999 PGA Tour and enjoys 12 PGA Tour victories; two Buy.com Tour victories; and even though he was sidelined for 10 weeks in 2000 with back problems, he rebounded with his 12th Tour victory at the Buick Challenge. Only two other active players have achieved as many wins in their 20's as David:Tiger Woods and Phil Mickelson.

The Story: The Stadium's seventeenth hole has seen its share of tragi-comedy, heroics, and red-faced embarrassment. Len Mattiace, on the brink of his first Tour victory in 1998, airmailed his tee shot over the green. One year later, David Duval birdied the hole in the final round of the 1999 Players Championship to cement his victory.

<u>The Secret</u>: This cyclopean creation by Dye wasn't the first island green, but it is by far the most famous, and the most lethal, especially on a windy day. There is nowhere to run, nowhere to hide on this man-eating midget. The target is only 121 yards from the blue tees and 97 yards from the white pegs. But this isn't about yardage. It's about confidence and guts. "I wanted to test the best players in the world emotionally as well as physically and mentally" was the Marquis de Sod's rationalization for his wicked bit of watery stagecraft. Mission accomplished.

Only the strong—and the prepared—will survive.

On The Links

Part I

Discussion from an Executive point of view

On The Links
Part I

Acme and Ajax had just signed a deal to merge their two components companies, both leaders in the industry. A full announcement to the public and the employees of both companies was planned for two days hence.

Stan, the CEO of Acme, had arranged a golf outing with Kent, the CEO of Ajax and a key executive from each company. Jeri, Vice President of Operations for Ajax, and Mark, Vice President of Sales for Acme had met each other but had not spent a lot of time together. For the Acme-Ajax merger to achieve the lofty goals outlined during the merger discussions the four people playing golf today were going to have to work well as a team.

In Stan's opinion the two companies had complementary strengths. Ajax had an excellent reputation in the marketplace. Their quality and delivery record had made them number three in the market and their market share was growing steadily. Acme , on the other hand, was number one in the marketplace because of their marketing and sales expertise.

Stan was first up and hit a solid drive that, though long, landed in the second cut of rough on the right. He commented to the group, "As my South Carolina friends would say, my towards was off." The other three laughed and the initial tension was broken.

Stan and Kent, the two CEO's, rode together in the golf cart. Kent said, "Stan, that South Carolina saying is humorous, but it got me to thinking about how sure we are that the "towards" of our new company strategy is "on".

Stan replied, "Kent, you and I are pretty clear on where we want to take the new company. During our negotiations it became apparent to me that while you and I understand the scope of what needs to be done, our top teams may not be as clear on the new company's direction. For example, Mark appears to have strong feelings on what needs to be done around products and markets, but I'm not sure if Jeri shares those feelings. Manufacturing and sales are going to need to be in sync to meet the growth we committed to in the merger."

Stan and Kent agreed on the necessity of getting Mark and Jeri to begin talking about the strategy for the new company, and this golf outing seemed like the perfect opportunity to raise some of the key issues for discussion.

The group had fun the rest of the day talking about their "towards" when it came to hitting, chipping or putting. Both Stan and Kent used every opportunity to tie the "towards" to open discussion around the possibilities for the new company.

During a refreshment break at the 9th hole, Mark did a nice job of summarizing some insights he had gained during the round.

He said that playing good golf and running a company seemed to have a lot in common. The clearer you were in what you intended to accomplish the easier it would be to coordinate the activities to make it happen. In golf it was getting your grip, stance, and swing to work in harmony. In business it was getting your operations, marketing, and sales systems working in harmony. Jeri made it clear that she had been able to get the quality, cost, and delivery equation working well at Ajax and Mark felt her approach made sense. He also felt there were a lot of opportunities in the market, and was concerned about meeting goals if they tried to be all things to all people.

Jeri jumped in to support Mark's points saying, "Combining the products the two companies currently manufacture will become a production nightmare. Fortunately, it is clear Mark feels that rationalizing the product line is both necessary and doable. The question for me is how to do the product rationalization so that it maximizes both market needs and manufacturing capabilities."

Stan and Kent were pleased. The issues Mark and Jeri had surfaced were the right issues.

Stan commented, "You two have confirmed what Kent and I have been thinking also. Our executive team needs to have a clear and common picture of the scope and direction of this new company including the products we will and will not offer, the markets we will and will not serve, and the way we will, and will not, do business."

Kent added, "We know there are different points of view among the top team members and we need those differing points of view surfaced. It is imperative to our success that the best thinking of the full executive team is explored so that the hard decisions about what to focus our time and resources on can be made. We have engaged an experienced merger consulting firm to work with us to develop a total integration plan over the next ninety days. The first step will be to hammer out a clear strategy for the combined company. Both of you, Mark and Jeri, will be on the strategy formulation task force. You and the other executives will have only three weeks to create the new strategy. The "towards" of the new company will be in your hands.

Chapter Four
GRIP

DIRECTION, *Discipline, DamnfastDelivery*
Getting It Right in the Integration Strategy and Product Roadmap

Getting A Grip

Professional golfers take into consideration direction, distance, and trajectory in preparing to execute a shot. They may have in-depth discussions with their caddies on the exact type of shot to hit based on the course layout and weather conditions. They will employ different club selections at St. Andrews in Scotland than when the greens are hard and the rough is deep at the U.S. Open.

Regardless of course conditions, the golfer's fundamental skills and techniques are still the key determinants of success. For that reason golf professionals will advise that a strong foundation, starting with the proper grip, is critical to hitting a good shot. In mergers the same advice holds true. The establishment of a clear and definitive direction that the combined executive team will commit to, a good grip, is critical to the ultimate success of the merger.

Mergers that avoid the 83% failure rate have all provided a clear statement of how the merged companies will compete with the marketplace, rather than with each other, to win. This statement of direction, which will be referred to in this book as the integration strategy, provides the fundamental framework for nearly all decision-making as the integration plans are developed. The integration strategy is developed by key functional executives from both companies working as a strategic planning team within the integration project structure.

To create this integration strategy, executives must engage in candid discussions early on. They will have different perceptions about their past and present business environment and what needs to be done to capitalize on the future. Surfacing these views allows for a reasoned exploration of the information that led to these different perceptions. It will also foster a common understanding of the impact these differences will have on future decisions. A tremendous amount of time and energy is saved by fearlessly attacking these issues early, and the probability of the success of the integration increases exponentially. If this step is ignored, well-meaning executives can end up providing conflicting directions to the organization, causing valuable resources to spend unnecessary effort and money on the wrong activities.

The most effective integration strategies are not large documents but they do contain clear priorities on the efficient use of all organizational resources. Clarity on the core competencies needed to deploy against specific products and markets, establishes the foundation for rapid and disciplined construction of a business model that will make the new company fly past the competition.

Just as important as discussing perceptions about future product and market direction, is the imperative for the executive team to surface their similarities and differences of approach regarding customers, sales channels, development cycles, and the organization culture in an equally frank manner. One method to surface these questions quickly and thoroughly is a Competitive Scan that covers a broad range of issues around the business environment, the competitive environment, governmental regulations, potential disruptive technologies, major strengths, and key vulnerabilities for each of the companies.

The objective of the Competitive Scan, an example of which can be viewed in Chapter Seven, is to prompt discussion on the right issues and to gain consensus among the executive team on specific business assumptions that will drive future decisions.

The results of the Competitive Scan provides focus for the scope of products and services to be offered; the markets they will be sold into; and, the core competencies that will be required to achieve the revenues and profits within that product and market scope. It takes into account the basic beliefs around people and how work gets done, and outlines the behaviors that will be required to take the company forward most effectively. It begins to assess which current beliefs and behavior patterns within each company should be capitalized on, left alone, or modified to ensure market leadership.

> Deliver the *right* product to the *right* customer at the *right* price at the *right* time

The top executive should pay particular attention to the human dynamics of his or her executive team as it comes together for the first time. Though politeness is comfortable, the overly-polite behavior that tends to prevail in these first meetings makes it difficult to get accurate and complete information on the table, especially information about the products and markets that are the very purpose of the gathering. The top executives must set the expectation immediately that there will be full disclosure inside these sessions if the deal is to succeed. This is not an easy request to comply with after years of hiding critical market and business information from the very competitors who now sit at the same table.

It will be necessary to push through the discomfort of not knowing what to expect from each other, and the fear of what it means to each person professionally if there is to be an understanding of the passions, ideals, and commitment of key people. Those executives willing to persevere through the discomfort will see their team build a strong and collaborative relationship, and demonstrate excitement about the possibilities ahead.

After each company has fully disclosed what it is, what it has, and how it does business, exploration can begin on ways to engage interpersonally and operationally to get the value that the deal projected.

Once the executive team is clear on the direction the business should take, it can begin enlisting the rest of their organization to help.

"A key to sound shots is to set the club in good position at the top of the swing. Then you don't have to make compensations for it on your downswing."
Tom Watson

Opening Moves

As soon as the strategic planning team has nailed down the shape of the competitive environment and the products and markets they will throw against it, they must begin to assemble the task forces that will deploy the operational and support systems. This will generally take the form of Integration Planning Task Forces composed of management talent from each company whose charter is to research and recommend best practices to achieve the new direction as rapidly as possible. Done well, the integration strategy, backed by the task force work, enables the organization to operate as one seamless company with near lightning speed.

To bring accountability and discipline to the planning effort, an effective project manager must be identified immediately to guide, direct, and charter the integration planning task forces. These task forces are often functional in design and will be responsible for assessing the "as-is" of that function in each company, moving quickly to the "to-be" thinking for the combined company. There is need for extreme clarity and communication with these task forces up front relative to their roles and responsibilities, and how they fit into the rest of the integration planning effort. The project structure outlined by the executive team will spell out the interim decision-making structures, stakeholders and their information needs, and ground rules for the integration planning process.

The establishment of task forces also increases the speed and reliability of information about the progress of the integration. Awareness sessions for 100% of the organization gets a critical mass of people on board with what to expect from the coming changes. It is important to clearly and widely communicate what is expected of everyone in the coming months in order to put this plan in place quickly and effectively.

<u>Watch The Traps</u>

The most likely causes of failure at the Direction stage of integration, if they are left unattended, include:

Failure to consider a new strategy for a new situation
No sense of urgency
Lack of common decision-making processes
Lack of strong criteria for decision-making
Short-sighted thinking
Turf protection
Bids for power
Lack of true risk analysis
Unwillingness to commit necessary time and resources for the transition
Failure to plan and implement against a specific timeframe

On The Links

Part II

Discussion from an Executive point of view

On The Links
Part II

As the CEO's of Acme and Ajax continued putting the pieces in place to bring the two companies together into one successful new company, they sought out a key player who had the credibility and skills to make sure all the moving parts of this integration came together on time with the least resistance.

Kyle, Human Resource Manager for Acme, had a strong track record of bringing projects in on time and a reputation for being able to turn conflict into constructive action. In addition, Kyle had demonstrated a good feel for the business issues and understood how all of the functions needed to work together to achieve their objectives.

Both CEO's agreed he would be an excellent integration project manager.

Kyle was excited, nervous and a bit overwhelmed. As the designated integration project manager he knew he would either be the hero or the heel in very short order. The merger consultants Stan had hired seemed to know their business and had laid out a good project plan. They had also made it clear that they would be right there to coach at each step, but that all decisions would be made by the executive team. He had seen them in action during the initial strategy sessions and appreciated the process they used to keep the group focused on the right issues, resulting in a strategic statement that all of the top team could support enthusiastically.

The next challenge was to get the new business and organization structures designed to align with the strategy. Kyle invited Adam, COO of the former Acme, for a round of golf. In addition to Adam, Kyle invited Flak and Dorothy from the merger consulting firm, to round out the foursome. It was important that Adam be on board for the challenges facing them as they built one new company, Alstar, out of the two former competitors.

Flak had suggested that instead of getting golf carts they hire caddies from the club to allow them more face time as they walked the course. Cadish was a highly respected caddie who had played the Pro circuit. He knew the course well and had the reputation of being able to evaluate his player's strengths and weaknesses rapidly. It was not unusual for a player to lower his score by three to five strokes when Cadish was coaching him. Cadish was paired with Adam.

Adam was looking forward to the outing. He loved the game of golf even though his heavy schedule often limited him to playing once a week during the season. He was looking forward to a break from the intense activities over the past few months as the negotiations of the merger concluded. He was also interested in getting to know the two consultants that had been contracted to take them through the integration of the two companies. His experience with consultants in the past had been mixed.

Cadish watched Adam carefully on the practice tee. Adam had pretty sound fundamentals but appeared to have a tendency to try to kill the ball. The extra effort when going for distance tended to make his long shots erratic. Adam's short irons and putting were pretty good for someone with a 15 handicap. Cadish's goal was to get Adam around the course under 85. In addition to the satisfaction of helping Adam improve his game, he knew that if he was able to accomplish his goal a nice tip would be forthcoming .

The first hole was uneventful. All four players made par. The difficulty on the second hole, a 170 yard par 3, was keeping the ball below the hole because of the slope and break of that green. Adam asked for his 5 iron. Cadish suggested that with the hole conditions and Adam's style, a 6 iron might work better. Adam insisted on the 5 iron. He hit a nice shot just to the right of the pin about 30 feet from the hole with a wicked left to right break. Cadish indicated, given the position of the ball and the slope of the green, Adam should lightly putt three feet to the left of the hole just to get the ball rolling, and then let gravity do the work. This time Adam listened. Gravity did its work and Adam's putt dropped into the cup. When he beat par on the hole Adam decided Cadish knew his business and that he could benefit from following his caddy's suggestions.

Further proof of Cadish's coaching value came seven holes later. A four hundred yard hole with a 60 degree dog leg to the right. A 250 yard drive goes right through the fairway putting the golfer in deep rough. Cadish advised Adam to hit his three wood just left of the pines rather than going for distance. A 220 yard drive to this position would give Adam a four or five iron to the green. Adam put a smooth swing on the ball and hit it within five yards of his intended target. A nice four iron to the green gave him a 20 foot putt for a birdie. Cadish again lined him up and Adam sank the putt. He had just played the front nine in 41, the best nine he had had all summer. Adam was in a great mood.

All four of them had a great afternoon and played some of their best golf ever. At the ninetieth hole over drinks they reflected on the afternoon.

Adam said, " You know I've never had the chance to play this course before. The rolling hills, deep rough, and undulating greens really had me worried. I thought if I broke 90 I would be a happy camper. With an 83 I'm ecstatic. "

Kyle echoed Adam's feelings and added, "Those caddies sure did help. They kept me relaxed and focused on my game. They gave me options on what and where to hit based on my skills and the conditions of the course. My concentration was better than it has ever been."

Dorothy said, "We are pleased you had that kind of experience. The reason Flak suggested using caddies was to give you a feeling of how we consult. Like our caddies knew this golf course, we know mergers. Like our caddies knew how to evaluate the golfers they were helping, we know how to evaluate the capabilities of the executives we are working with.

Developing the business structure, organization chart, and systems for the new company will be like playing on a golf course you have never seen before. Just as the caddies today suggested we use different clubs than we might normally use, or suggested playing the break on the green differently than we initially thought we should, we will make suggestions on how you can use your capabilities to address the different steps in integrating your merger in the most effective way."

Flak interjected, "You have put together a product, market, and core competency strategy that will be maximized if the structure and systems support them correctly. Just as form follows function, structure follows strategy. Adam, as the COO, you have a critical leadership role. The way you deployed your knowledge, skill, and attitudes in your current organization worked exceedingly well. As you work with the joint executive team to determine the business model that best fits the new strategy, you may have to deploy your capabilities in a slightly different way to be most effective. Just like our caddies today, if we ask you to consider a different approach we will communicate why the different approach will get better results."

Adam concluded, "I beat my handicap on a new and difficult course by listening to a caddie. I'm willing to capitalize on your merger experience to beat par on this deal. I'm looking forward to tackling the structure process."

BOOK TWO
THE GAME

Chapter Five
SET UP—<u>Discipline</u>

Structures, systems,
and decision-making

Hole: Durban Country Club
Location: Durban, Natal, South Africa
Architects: George Waterman, Laurie Waters

Golfer: Gary Player
Bio Snapshot: Born Gary Jim Player on November 1, 1935, in Johannesburg, South Africa he still resides in Johannesburg with his wife Vivienne, close to their six children and 11 grandchildren. Gary turned pro in 1953, and joined the PGA Tour in 1957. With 21 PGA Tour victories and 19 Senior PGA Tour victories he was dubbed variously the Black Knight, Mr. Fitness, and the International Ambassador of Golf. Gary is also a renowned golf architect with over 100 design projects located throughout the world. He has traveled more miles than any athlete in history, over 12 million.

The Story: Shadowed for years by the veil of apartheid, South Africa, after turning the page on its unfortunate past in the mid-1990s, entered the millennium as a thriving golf destination. All the ingredients for superlative golf are there: a congenial year-round climate, breathtaking natural beauty, and a strong golf heritage. The South African Open is older than the U.S. Open! The most highly regarded layout in South Africa is Durban Country Club, and Gary its most successful competitor, capturing the first of his *thirteen* South African Open victories at the club in 1956.

The Secret: Why is Hole 3 at Durban, in part, so critical to the success of a round? Robert Grimsdell summed it up perfectly: "The player is not shown everything at a glance, but is given the thrill of anticipation and uncertainty." A 513-yard march through a valley of dunes, the third hole is straight only in direction. The undulating fairway is complicated by a deep bunker on the left; the approach even more so, thanks to twin kidney-shaped bunkers. Push a shot past the elevated green and the bush owns the ball. Only the disciplined swing will accurately place the ball on the green.

Discipline, accuracy, and uncertainty—are complementary.

Chapter Five

SET UP

Direction, DISCIPLINE, *DamnfastDelivery*
Getting It Right in Structures, Systems, and Decision-making

Golfers put clubs in their bag that fit the type of course they will be playing. On a course known for high winds a golfer will change one or two clubs in order to maneuver the ball more effectively in the wind. A high altitude course will require the golfer to focus on clubs that will help control the accuracy. A long course with 450 to 480 yard par fours calls for clubs that maximize distance. Professional golfers would never approach a tournament without understanding the course and which clubs will provide them the greatest edge on that course.

In the same way, top executives in mergers recognize that their new company will require adjustments. How the company will be structured and which systems will support that structure are some of the "clubs in the bag" that may need adjustment. The strategy work will have provided an understanding of the course, and careful consideration can now be given to the best club combination.

Your staff will want to immediately fill in an organization chart with names and titles. Familiar faces and names. You will be tempted to do just that. It would be what is expected. It would be exactly the wrong thing to do.

The merger and its integration decisions have presented the organization with different business requirements and new market possibilities, as well as a broader talent pool to answer that challenge with. If you simply put the same names in the same boxes on an organization chart, your new organization will be based on past needs. It will be based on the experience of a singular organization, not taking into account the potential talent combinations available now.

Don't yield to the pressure to simply rearrange the deck chairs. Charter a team to work systematically on determining what business model or combination of business models will be best to implement the integration strategy. For example, if your growth requirements will cause some areas to grow faster than others or will vary greatly, a business unit model will work best. If manufacturing capabilities are what will set the new company apart from the competition, then a functional business model will work best. The question really is, what business model will allow the new company to meet and exceed its potential.

> *Set up dead square to the target line. Whether your stance is open like Raymond Floyd's or closed like Gary Player's—the shoulders have to be square.*

The team that works through the new business model question will be comprised of the top players from each company, the very executives who will most likely have to make this new enterprise work. Generally it is the vice presidents representing key functions such as marketing, sales, operations, finance, human relations, and R&D. Some of these same people will have been with you during the integration strategy discussions, but you will need to expand the business model team to incorporate a wider pool of thought leaders representing the functions.

What business model best fits the new organization's emerging needs? What criteria will be used to determine the best choice? The integration strategy and the success factors outlined in it would be a good place to start, especially if those success factors are translated into decision criteria through which all business model alternatives will have to pass.

Use of a good decision making process that is criteria based will force objectivity into the final decision. It will prevent, to a large degree, the politics, turf building, and bids for power that can occur.

Demand that the business model team test, test, and re-test the proposed alternatives against that decision criteria and not just their gut feel for the business. Gut feel is important and experience can provide useful guidance, but the decision needs ultimately to be made on supportable facts. These business model decisions will determine how resources are deployed in the organization.

Finally, when the business model is complete and the tension is almost unbearable, the executive can turn that task force loose on its next assignment....the one it has been waiting for...population of an organization chart. The team that has been functioning as the business model task force generally continues on as the organization structure task force.

Before the task force begins deliberation on the organization structure design, the people who sit on that team must know for sure where they, personally, are going to play. If they are unclear as to their placement in the organization, they will be engaged in necessary politics and maneuvering and will be unable to concentrate fully on the task at hand....where does everyone else go in the organization. It is important that the top layer of the organization is identified and announced just as the organization structure deliberations, not the business structure discussions, kick off. That top layer generally includes the CEO, CFO, COO, and their immediate reporting line.

Each name in the box on the organization chart must fulfill the clear and specific requirements of that position and be agreed to by consensus of the organization structure task force members. The organization chart is usually filled out for the two levels below the top executive's direct reports. Beyond that it will be the responsibility of the functional manager to complete an appropriate organization to achieve the strategic goals for that function.

The mandate to the organization structure task force members to make no premature promises about specific jobs still stands. There may be people who require reassurance in order to stay committed to the company, but you should be crystal clear before making an offer that this is the right resource for the new position, that it is in the best long term interests of the company to keep that resource, and that there is no other way to ensure that person stays. Any appointment at this stage should be considered rare.

There is no need to get caught in the money bargaining trap when retention is the question. When you meet and talk with key players you will find that their motivations are around recognition, challenge, succession, or autonomy more than around hard cash. Seriously interview them and find out what is making them tick right now. Assure them, not of a box on the chart, but of a chance to design their own future. You may have to sweeten the pot with a stay bonus or two, but be frugal. You need to spend a lot less than you might expect. The best people, the ones you really want to have with you, will be excited by the prospect of designing the future and will stay to see what can happen.

There are some key talents that you will want to hang on to, who are critical to the short or long term survival of the core business because they have proprietary knowledge, skills, or an influence network. It is important to find out what will keep that talent at home and what the urgency of an offer is, but remember the motivation to stay will have a great deal to do with being a part of something that matters.

There can be about two weeks between completion of the business model and the start of organization structure discussions, but delaying beyond that will cause momentum and interest to slip. When momentum and interest slip people focus inward on their "me issues" instead of outward on customer issues. "Me issues" are personal needs or fears about where you fit, what you will do, how your livelihood will be affected. Keep the heat turned up! Set time limits on how long the planning teams have for their tasks. For example, integration strategy discussions consume about six days of work interspersed over a three to four week period. The business model discussions can start immediately after the integration strategy is finalized and should be completed within three weeks. The organization structure discussions start soon after the business model is approved and should be completed within another three weeks.

Without missing a beat, the executive team and the project manager launch those critical systems teams that compare how business is done now in each function with how it should be done going forward. These system planning task forces, aligned around function and comprised of equal representation from each organization are chartered for approximately eight to ten weeks to carefully assess the best practices of each company to determine which should be kept, which should be modified, and which no longer are useful. They are populated by key managers and influencers most likely to play in the new organization.

The System Task Force charters include:

- Converting the integration strategy into a new set of operational procedures, processes, and measurements for each function

- Researching, comparing, and recommending the best possible operational scenarios for bringing best practices together

- Screening all recommendations against the integration strategy and the business model requirements

- Working collaboratively across functions for the greater good of the emerging organization

- Detailing a staged migration of the current processes to the ideal

While participating as a task force member, these managers will continue to oversee their current position responsibilities. They will spend from thirty to sixty percent of their effort on system task force work, the amount of time fluctuating on a week to week basis. This provides a perfect opportunity for managers to practice effective delegation and development of their people; to demonstrate their capability to respond to and effectively prioritize multiple initiatives; and to experience first hand what it takes to create and launch a viable new business.

One way to reinforce the importance of these system task forces is to bring them all together in one place as soon as you have identified them. This gathering also provides a forum to deliver the same message to everyone at the same time and to foster the speed, energy, and commitment needed to quick-start the integration planning process. It increases the feeling of the participants that they are no longer strangers from competing organizations, but experienced equals with value to offer to the new venture. Working together in one room surfaces turf battles, risks, cultural similarities and gaps faster, and reinforces the need for collaboration. It provides a controlled environment for key players to begin building invaluable relationships and networks they will need to run the business. It also allows the executives to assess these managers potential and how they will perform under pressure.

The room will vibrate with energy when you assemble that many good minds in one place and focus them on the possibilities associated with building a new business. Leveraging this energy properly will propel you through the critical integration planning period.

These task forces generally need to come together again halfway through their eight weeks of work to reinforce that everyone is still on the same page, and to provide recognition for the incredibly hard work they have been exhibiting.

In defining the new set of procedures, processes, and measures for each function, an efficient and effective method to gather information on the driving issues and questions under consideration is the use of standardized formats. These formats guide the task forces in quickly understanding the type of information and priorities required. Rather than spending energy creating the methods and questions to be used, the formats provide the vehicle and leave the task force members time and energy free for hard hitting discussions around the issues and opportunities presented. Examples of some of these formats can be viewed in Chapters 7, 8 and 9.

Common formats also provide a way of describing and reporting the data gathered so it can be easily assimilated and compared for decision-making or action planning by the executive team and the project manager. Two types of data you will want the task forces to compare in developing their integration plans are content data and context data. Content data will include such subjects as asset evaluation, risk assessment, operation rationalization, customer profiles, and benefits and conditions of employment. Context data will include such subjects as business strategy and structure, decision-making processes, communication strategies, cultural values, and recognition systems.

In addition to the best practice quest of these task forces in combining two separate functional areas into one, challenge them with digging out all of the revenue and cost potential for that function while they are at it. Require them to quantify everything.

There are many moving parts in an integration. Clarity on who plays which role and what the requirements are will go a long way to increasing the speed with which the task forces engage and produce the necessary information for decisions.

Specific actions you can take to ensure roles are clear and this work materializes cleanly include installing a project management process, a project structure, and a strong project manager as its champion.

An example of a disciplined project management process for system work might look like this:

1. Executives define the rules of engagement governing the project
2. A project manager is sanctioned

3. The project manager charters system task forces to analyze and gather data for best-practice recommendations on combining functional work
4. System task forces identify potential revenue and cost synergies and develop integration and migration plans
5. The executive team reviews, approves or revises plans, and provides guidance weekly through the project manager
6. The project manager monitors development of final recommendations to the executive team for implementation of the integration plans
7. The executive team approves final plans and authorizes implementation of the plans including schedules and budgets
8. The executive team disbands and recognizes the task forces and project manager, assigning the completed integration plans to the newly announced organization managers

Executives keep tight control of the integration activities, not by micro-managing, but by holding each of the project teams accountable for producing the results detailed in their charters, and by establishing clear rules of engagement. Rules of engagement govern not only the roles and responsibilities within the integration project structure, but the criteria for success of the integration, decision-making parameters for all groups, frequency of review of integration plans and processes, disband date for all groups, conflict resolution guidelines between and among groups, and general forms and formats to be used for documentation. An example of a project structure can be seen in Chapter Eight. The project manager is in daily contact with the task forces to ensure the appropriate information with sufficient detail is being focused on. A weekly exchange with the executive team provides guidance and decisions where needed.

When you involve the best people in planning your organization, provide them with high expectations and tools to move quickly, you can complete a thorough integration plan and be prepared to launch implementation of those plans within ninety days. You can even begin putting some of the task force recommendations in place prior to the end of the ninety day planning phase.

At the end of those ninety days the participants in the process are tired. They have been doing two full time jobs, getting the day to day results required in the business while integrating the merging organizations. Everyone wants to go back to "business as usual" and take a break. While a short breather is required for the task force, a breather is not an option for the top team. All members of the executive team will have initiatives and specific recommendations coming out of the task force plans that directly relate to their new areas of responsibility. If they let up right now people will relax back into comfortable, familiar, old patterns...the momentum will be lost and the implementation of all that hard work will be in jeopardy.

Prioritize the actions identified during the integration planning phase and push the focus to implementation. Capitalize on the momentum established during the fast paced ninety day integration process. People are expecting the changes that have been recommended to be implemented. They will scrutinize the next thirty days closely to see if what they heard is going to actually come into being.

The managers who helped design the new organization are receptive to the changes they have helped design, and are anxious to see them put to work. As part of the task force, they made specific recommendations on what should be done and their credibility and commitment are both on hook when they return to every day operations. They will be watching carefully to see that the executive team moves forward with the implementation quickly.

Watch The Traps

Traps in Discipline that are most likely to derail a well-started process include:

Lack of accountability for all groups

Lack of precise expectations between task forces and the executive team

Failure to get the right people involved on the task forces

Neglecting to require collaboration among the teams during planning

Leading teams to believe they have input into who goes where in the new organization structure

Neglecting to communicate with the organization regularly on the status of the project and the process

Lack of understanding about what's appropriate to communicate during the process

Making promises behind the scenes and the building of individual empires

Not using clear criteria around competencies to match people to positions

On The Links

Part III

Discussion from an Executive point of view

On The Links
Part III

Along with the final announcement of the Acme and Ajax merger, had come the announcement that the new name would be Alstar. A new logo was in the works that would include both the old Acme and Ajax names and logo's at the bottom for continuing brand recognition and customer loyalty until Alstar could demonstrate its unity of product and service to the marketplace.

Kyle, the integration manager, had arranged a golf outing with Alstar's newly appointed executives and the functional system task forces as a fun reward for the hard work the task forces had put in over the past four weeks. Kyle was in the foursome that included Alstar's new C-level team: Stan, CEO; Adam, COO; and, Joe, CFO.

Kyle was impressed with the work that had been done up to this point, and wanted the executives to support and encourage the work because he knew that the real pressures on the task forces lay ahead. Kyle hoped to have the opportunity while they were playing to impress on Stan, Adam, and Joe the critical role they needed to play in the next six weeks to ensure the synergies and initiatives coming out of the task forces were backed by solid integrated implementation plans.

For the first three holes the group concentrated on the game. They blended pretty well as a team. Joe was clearly the best golfer in the group with a 9 handicap, and while Kyle had grown up playing golf he had not really played much over the last few years because of business and family pressures. Stan, given his once a week outings during the season, was strong but erratic. Adam played golf in the company league to keep a pulse on the operations, but considered himself only a "happy hacker".

They were all laughing and joking coming off the fourth green. Adam said, " Well, I didn't contribute much on this hole but I was a great cheerleader." Joe piped in, "That's the advantage of a scramble over other types of golf. You get to rely on your partners to get you out of trouble."

After the four holes the group was two under par and comfortable with each other's play. Joe started the ball rolling around business by saying, " I was pleased to see the task force ideas around cost reductions. My quick math totaled more synergy dollars than we promised the street. I hope we can pull it off."

Adam reinforced Joe's comments by adding, " I was impressed with the presentations, too. I'm amazed at how quickly they were able to surface the critical issues that need to be resolved in order for this merger to work the way we all want it to work. The task force briefings we have been getting on a weekly basis gave a flavor for what was going to happen over these two days of presentations, but the level of analysis was even more extensive and detailed than I had imagined. I can tell you I am much more comfortable than I was two days ago that we definitely can pull this off."

Kyle added, "Adam, remember on the fourth hole when you made the point about being a cheerleader. You, Stan, and Joe have done a great job of cheerleading the task forces over the last four weeks. Your vigilance and focus about getting all of the information on the table helped break some major barriers down."

Stan piped up, "Just like this scramble, you never know where the help is going to come from, do you? In the presentation yesterday on distribution rationalization, there was a lot of concern about how to reduce the distribution sites by 50%. A real thorny problem, but John Fredricks from your operations group, Adam, made a great presentation and outlined some very realistic alternatives. I'm looking forward to digging into the details on that issue. As these task forces work we are not only hearing some solid thinking, but we are also getting exposure to some excellent talent I didn't know we had."

After spending time moving about the clubhouse after the outing in order to congratulate the different task forces on their results, Stan reflected on the integration effort to this point. He summarized some of the things he had seen and heard in the two days of presentations by saying, "We are attempting a full merger. That is to say we want to take the best practices of both Acme and Ajax and blend them into a new, stronger entity where the whole is greater than the sum of its parts. The use of tasks forces comprised of leaders from both organizations had me worried. I felt that we would have major "turf protection" problems. The presentations over the past two days calmed my concerns. We saw solid thinking, reasonable approaches, and in-depth analysis. I was impressed with the way you all were able to openly identify and then agree on both the good and the bad aspects of the current systems and procedures. Opinions were backed up with supporting information, and individual lobbying was kept in perspective of the needs of the whole organization. Like the scramble today where your teams collectively beat the score one individual could have achieved alone, your task forces are coming up with solutions that are far better than what individuals could have done alone."

Stan continued, "We now have a strategy that provides focus for the new company. We have a business model and the top few levels of the organization structure that will be in place shortly. Over the past month your task forces have been adding the type of detail to the implementation plans that will make certain the strategy and structure are successful. It has been an intense four weeks and you have done an exceptional job. Now, we have to keep that positive pressure on and finish with strength. You will get more information in tomorrow's session so that you can re-direct your plans where necessary and continue to move forward. Thank you, each and every one, for your work to date. Keep it up!"

Adam echoed Stan's optimism, and added, "Building this new company provides us with a challenge. The process we have used has helped us keep rumors under control, and to get information to everyone quickly. The strategy, product roadmap, business model, and organizational structure, and now the best-practice thinking around systems, gives us a strong, clear focus as we implement your plans over the coming months. It is amazing that it is only forty-five days into the integration process and we are this far along. My confidence level is high that by the end of ninety days we will have a high level of agreement on what the company needs to look like, feel like, and operate like in order for us to beat our competition."

Kyle was pleased with the results of the golf outing. The enthusiasm and understanding exhibited by the executive team made him feel comfortable the tough issues that had to be addressed would be addressed in the right way.

BOOK TWO
THE GAME

Chapter Six
SWING—<u>DamnfastDelivery</u>

Leadership, leverage, and energy points

Hole: Bethpage State Park Golf Club (Black)
Location: Farmingdale, NY
Architect: A.W. Tillinghast, Rees Jones

Golfer: Sam Snead
Bio Snapshot: Born Samuel Jackson Snead on May 27, 1912, in Hot Springs, VA, he turned pro in 1934, and joined the PGA Tour in 1937. Sam amassed eighty-one PGA Tour victories (the all time leader) and 14 Senior PGA victories. One of the founders of the Senior PGA Tour in 1980, he is a member of the PGA Hall of Fame and World Golf Hall of Fame. He made an appearance in 2000 at the British Open at St. Andrews for the Champion's Challenge, and served as honorary starter at the Masters Tournament along with Byron Nelson.

<u>The Story</u>: In the Bible, Beth'phage, or "House of Figs," is located between Jericho and Jerusalem. For the overconfident, the unprepared, or simply those easily intimidated by golf on a grand scale, the Black Course at Bethpage State Park on Long Island is located not an hour's drive east of New York City, but somewhere between Purgatory and Hades. The fifth hole is arguably the best hole on the course and possibly the finest two-shotter on the impressive resume of A.W. Tillinghast, a golden age architect. Too bad Sam Snead didn't stick around to see for himself. During an exhibition on the Black Course in 1940, Snead is reported to have stalked off the course in disgust after his second shot sailed over the green into oblivion at the par-5 fourth.

<u>The Secret</u>: "The finishing holes [of a course] decide more matches, ruin more rounds, produce more joy and suffering, and thus get more attention. In many cases, the last holes on a course were the first holes the architect 'saw' when he walked the raw terrain. He knew to save the best for last."—George Peper

Stay the Course!

Chapter Six

SWING

Direction, Discipline, DAMNFASTDELIVERY
Leveraging the Predictability of People and the Energy Points Created

Good golfers discipline themselves to follow a disciplined routine every time they approach a shot. The primary benefit of a set routine is that it allows the golfer to mentally evaluate the subtle differences each shot presents. A ball setting up high in the grass requires a slight modification in swing from one nestled deep in the grass. The better the golfer is at anticipating and executing those slight modifications, the higher the probability of posting a low score.

Executives that follow a disciplined process during an integration will have time to evaluate the subtle differences their particular merger presents and make smart adjustments.

Elements of a Disciplined Process

- A workable decision-making structure specific to the integration
- A dedicated, credible project manager
- Diverse, knowledgeable task forces
- A project approach to activities and timelines
- Accountability for results

Let's examine each of these elements in a bit more detail:

The Project Structure

The overriding necessity is to deploy an interim decision-making structure for the ninety day integration period that will oversee all of the moving parts. Generally this will take the form of a project structure which includes an executive steering committee, an integration team of senior executives, a project manager, and functional task forces, all of which are governed by clear rules of engagement. The businesses still must be run concurrently with the intense task of integrating two distinct organizations into one. Further expansion of a project structure is shown in Chapter Eight.

Speed comes from using a rigorous process that drives all the integration decisions and actions along a critical path that is monitored and championed by the executives in the project structure.

The Project Manager

The job of project manager is in many ways a thankless job and in many ways the best job in the world. The project manager is the pivotal communication link for the entire merger process. All information, decisions, considerations, and documents go through the project manager's hands. He or she is the arbiter of the process and acts as mentor and coach to the executives, the task force members, and the organization.

While all decisions ultimately remain with the executive team, the project manager tees them up and molds them to forms that are easy to digest. It is a heady responsibility. And an exhausting one. To carry the weight of the integration of two organizations is an arduous task indeed. In addition, the project manager shepherds, coaxes, cajoles and pressures the executives into making timely decisions and the task forces into submission of rich and accurate details in sync with the critical path of the project plan.

The meeting of deadlines and the assurance of the quality of task force information is laid directly at the project manager's feet. The pressure is intense. Done well, the reward is incredible as the plans unfold into a new and more vibrant organization in less time than anyone in the organization would have considered possible.

The Project Task Forces

The task forces are generating information for consideration by the executives on subjects such as: what processes should drive each function, how are the requirements of the integration plan resourced, what are the cost and revenue implications of the strategy, what competencies are required to pull it off, what interdependencies are crucial between functions, how does the competitive environment impact the process, and what best practices should be maintained.

Task force team leaders are pushing their teams for completion of prioritized initiatives that describe, in excruciating but necessary detail, those actions that must be taken in order to seamlessly blend two organizations into one. Once the teams are launched at the start of the project, they must be required to meet on a regular schedule and report weekly to the executive team through the project manager on their progress. The executive team must be free to continue to conduct the business of doing business, yet be sufficiently involved to feel confident that the type of organization they envisioned is being built.

The project structure will ensure weekly guidance on the degree of fit between the integration strategy and the thinking being done in the task forces. Their work is communicated to the executive team weekly in an executive summary format. The project manager has seen to it that the summary carries sufficient information to allow the executives to understand the thinking behind any changes well enough to provide guidance, but not so much detail that the executives are lost in the details of the planning

The Project Approach

A strong project provides for regular meetings and communication points between and among all the moving pieces of the project. The steering committee and project manager will communicate daily informally, and weekly in a formal setting to view the work coming up from the task forces and to create

decisions that push back down. The project manager will communicate daily with the project team leads and accept formal
submissions weekly on standardized reporting forms. The task
force leads will talk daily with their teams and work on the
phone in a team conference call weekly. The task forces, in
total, need to come together face to face every third week, min-
imally, in order to maintain the understanding, consistency and
speed of the work. These face to face meetings perpetuate the
ongoing commitment of all members of the teams and provide
energy to regularly "jump start" the level of motivation of the
team members and the organization as they see progress.

The rest of the organization will need to receive weekly updates
on the progress of the integration. They know that members of
the organization are away at offsite meetings and working
together in teams and they want to know what they are up to.
The project manager will draft a communication to the organization twice a week. For example, on Monday the communication would include any new initiatives that have a final decision
for action from the steering committee, and on Friday it would
include answers to questions about the integration that have
bubbled up from the organization. The design and delivery of
these communiqués is an art in itself. How much do you tell?
In what form? Exactly when do you tell what? Delicate stuff,
this.

The Project Accountability for Results

The race to the finish in ninety days or less heightens the pressure and excitement as the task force plans begin to yield actual numbers and dollars. Synergies are the word of the day. Teams strive to push their numbers up each week as they exhaustively research the possibilities and report them to the executive team. The project manager has an invaluable job here in helping the teams to think in terms of dollars and numbers on subjects that often are historically only talked of in conceptual terms.

The task forces are responsible for creating the new processes and the culture that will embody the emerging organization. They also are responsible for describing how the success of those plans will be measured, in concrete terms. There is often much groaning and gnashing of teeth at this point as teams recognize the responsibility inherent in the task, and that the organization will be holding them accountable for describing success accurately. The ante goes up considerably during the final forty-five days of the project. Excitement goes up. Anxiety goes up. Anticipation goes up.

Watch The Traps

Those things that are most likely to slow down the organization's energy and ability to change include:

- Executives failing to demonstrate and require a continuing focus on the customer during change
- Perceptions that there are no strong decisions being made
- Letting the process and project deadlines slide even a little
- No visible changes
- Managers hiding in their own functional unit or sniping at their peers in other functions
- Unmanaged fear of the heightened emotions displayed during an integration

CLEATS, CLUBS, AND GOLF CARTS

BOOK THREE
CLEATS, CLUBS, AND GOLF CARTS

CHAPTER SEVEN
Tools for <u>Direction</u>

Chapter Seven
Tools for Direction

In this and the next two chapters, explanations of tools that can help achieve the results you would like to see in Direction, Discipline, and DamnfastDelivery will include specific examples as well as the purpose, timing, and level of executive involvement required for their success.

The results of using the tools provided in this chapter include: identification of the cultural, financial, and decision deal breakers; a true case assessment of the joint competitive position; familiarity with the values, culture, and leadership styles that are currently in place; and, a relatively accurate assessment of the capabilities necessary for success in your marketplace.

Direction Tools are designed to gather information in sufficient quantity and with sufficient accuracy to enable the executive team to make intelligent and timely decisions about where it should expend its energy and resources. They also are designed to help the executive team communicate their thinking and decisions clearly and cleanly to the organization.

These tools can include:

- Competitive Scan
- Integration Strategy Statement
- Product Roadmap

Competitive Scan

Purpose: Provide all participants the opportunity to compare market knowledge, gather accurate competitive information, and assess the true combined market opportunities and threats

Timing: Immediately upon closing

Setting: Face-to-face offsite

Level: Senior executives from each company

Questions and issues that are considered in developing an Integration Strategy and a Product Roadmap:

COMPETITORS
- Who are major direct and indirect competitors and what is their competitive advantage?
- What significant changes can you expect within your competition during your strategic timeframe (18-24 months)?
- What organizations do you expect to begin competing directly with you in the strategic timeframe?
- What entirely new forms of competition do you expect within the strategic timeframe?
- How should your current and potential offering be positioned in the marketplace to maximize barriers to entry from your competition?

STRENGTHS AND WEAKNESSES
- What specific strengths and weaknesses does your new organization expect to have compared to both your major direct and indirect competitors?
- What specific products and markets, if any, should you avoid based upon your relative strengths and weaknesses, compared to your direct and indirect competitors?

CUSTOMER AND MARKETPLACE ENVIRONMENT
- Using your major customer groups, answer the questions:
  - What is the market size?
  - What are the trends?
  - What are the implications of those trends?
  - What new strategic alliances should be considered during the next 18 months to enhance your competitive advantage?

GROWTH AND RETURN EXPECTATIONS
- What criteria do you use to measure success now and how should you measure it in the future?
- What are your specific expectations for growth and return within your strategic timeframe?
- What other specific objectives do you want to achieve over the next 18 months?

Integration Strategy Statement

Purpose: Clear articulation of the scope and direction the com-
         bined organization intends to pursue
Timing: Within two weeks of the start of the Competitive Scan
Setting: Second face-to-face offsite
Level: Senior executives from each company

Example of a completed Integration Strategy

During the next **three years** we will fill the basic need (needs) of the **Electronic Visual communication business**

We will serve **existing** education, business, government, and OEM markets **as well as new** dynamic signage, digital cinema and consumer markets.

We will serve these chosen markets with products that have the **common characteristics** of being electronic, using display content from other sources, and with the capability to output large format display.

We will build on our key strengths in:
        Generating product solutions that the customer wants
        Intelligent application of technology
        Product design
        Strategic supplier relationships

Our thrust for growth will be **current markets with current product characteristics** and **new markets with modified products.**

We will achieve top line growth of (x\$ in 2001), (x\$ in 2002), and (x\$ in 2003); and will increase our earnings per sale each year.

Example of a Product Roadmap

Purpose: Specific description of combined product line plans (which products will play in which markets in what timeframe)

Timing: Output of the Scan and Strategy work

Setting: Second face-to-face offsite

Level: Senior executives from each company

PRODUCTS

			CURRENT	MODIFIED	NEW
M A R K E T S	C U R R E N	Retail Banks U.S.	-eCentral 1X -ECentral 2X -Consulting -Cross Selling Existing Products 1	-Central -Local 2.0 -Integrated Product 3	✕
	E X T E N D E D	International Banks U.K. S. Africa	-eCentral 1X -ECentral 2X -Consulting -Cross Selling Existing Products 2	-eCentral -Local 2.0 for International Banking 5	✕
	N E W	Click & Mortar Retailing U.S., Canada & EMEA Insurance	-eCentral 1X -ECentral 2X -Consulting -Cross Selling Existing Products 4	-eCentral -Local 2.0 for Retailing 6	✕

☐ First 12 months

▨ End of 24 months

BOOK THREE
CLEATS, CLUBS, AND GOLF CARTS

CHAPTER EIGHT
Tools for <u>Discipline</u>

Chapter Eight
Tools for Discipline

Ironically, one of the ways to gain speed during integration is to slow down. Slow down long enough to bring together the best thinking, to increase the involvement and input of a broad spectrum of the organization, to focus the energy of change on the right priorities, and to be attentive to the timeliness and accuracy of decisions.

Just as the *Tools for Direction* detail the scope of the merged company's long-term potential, *Tools for Discipline* detail the scope of the short-term merger integration project that will transition the organization into its intended future. Attention at the front end of integration ensures that critical people, processes, and information don't fall through the crack in either the project details or the critical day to day operations.

These tools can include:

- Project Decision-Making Structure
- Rules of Engagement
- Team Charters

Sample Project Decision-Making Structure

Purpose: Appropriate checks and balances required to assure the plan will accomplish the synergies promised at the inception of the deal, make sure key players are intimately knowledgeable of plans and in a position to challenge or approve conclusions, to get best thinking of those involved in the function, and ensure commitment to implementation of the plan, clear understanding of who is making the integration decisions

Timing: End of second strategy session

Setting: Face-to-face

Level: Senior executives from each company

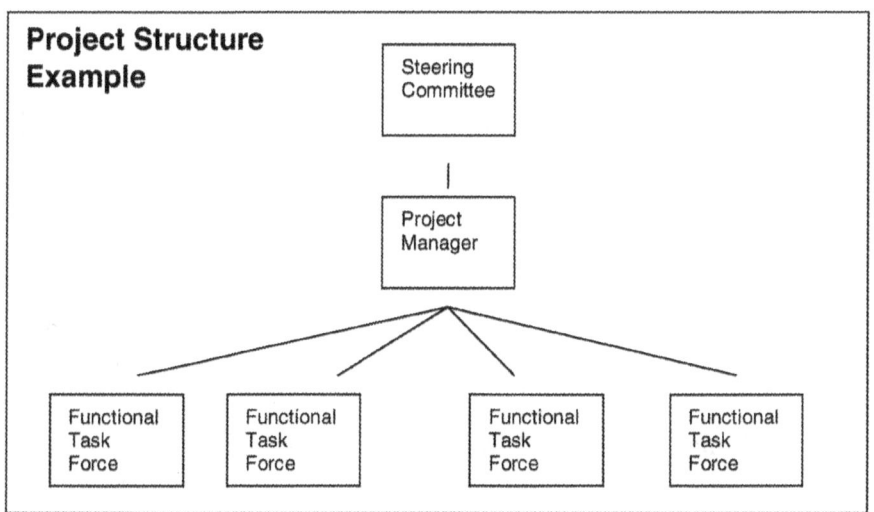

Sample Rules of Engagement

Purpose: In addition to expanding on the details of the project structure roles, provide guidance on decision-making autonomy for all groups, detail participation, contribution and communication expectations and conflict resolution methods

Timing: Completed at time of agreement on a project decision-making structure

Setting: Face-to-face

Level: Senior executives from each company

Rules of Engagement
GENERALLY DEFINED DUTIES

<u>Steering Committee:</u>
> Define the expected results and constraints
> Provide direction and support as required to the project manager and task forces
> Review and approve all task force recommendations
> Resolve conflict when necessary

<u>Project Manager:</u>
> Manage integration project to critical project path and timelines
> Provide ongoing communication between and among project structure groups
> Provide coaching and guidance to steering committee and task forces
> Monitor the weekly submission of required forms, including timeliness, content quality, and appropriateness
> Communicate project progress to the organization weekly
> Synthesize task force work into weekly executive summary for the steering Committee
> Facilitate steering committee meetings

Task Forces:
>Develop detailed plans to achieve the integration objectives
>
>Make recommendations to the Steering Committee for implementation plans and priorities
>
>Communicate with and take direction from Steering Committee
>
>Report progress to Steering Committee weekly
>
>Consistently communicate project progress to the organization

DECISION-MAKING LATITUDE

Steering Committee:
>Final decisions on all integration planning recommendations and activities

Project Manager:
>Recommendations on task force progress and resource needs

Task Forces may make:
>Recommendations only on improvements or changes in processes, structure, systems, training, and implementation of integration plans

APPROVAL PROCESS OUTLINE

1) Task forces identify potential synergies and develop initial integration plan recommendation to the Steering Committee

2) Project manager prepares an Executive Summary of combined task force work for the Steering Committee consideration

3) Steering Committee reviews, approves or disapproves, and provides guidance for continuing work on the plan

4) Task forces develop final recommendations for implementation of the integration plans

5) Steering Committee approves (or disapproves) plan and authorizes implementation, schedule, budget, etc

6) Steering Committee disbands task forces, then project manager, then the Steering Committee itself once plans are transitioned to the new functional managers

Sample Task Force Charter

Purpose: Set clear expectations on roles, task scope and responsibility, output, process, timing, and decision parameters
Timing: Within two weeks of strategy completion
Setting: Face-to-face kickoff of process
Level: Functional managers

Task Force Charter

Team Name:
Team Members:
Roles and Contingency Planning: Task Force Lead, Scribe, Logistics Planning and Communication, Documentation and Archives, External Facilitator
Task Force Purposes: ("Why do we exist" and what purpose are we to accomplish in the integration?)
Prioritized Synergies/Results: (Specific initiatives this team will create and develop for the integration including specific steps to achieve the results required by the strategy)
Parameters: (What can change, what cannot)
Reporting/Communication: (Updates, how often, and to whom)
Logistics: (How this Task Force will meet, how often, location, possible resource needs, etc.)

Example of Purpose Statements for Task Force Charters

Strategy Task Force Purpose:
- Understand implications of proposed strategy
    o Relative to current systems/models at each site
    o Relative to specific project team focus
- Align all metrics driven initiatives to strategy (revenue & cost)

Systems Task Force Purpose:
- performance gap analysis of existing operations against new integration strategy and agreed business structure
- Propose metrics driven initiatives to fill the gaps (revenue & cost)

BOOK THREE

CLEATS, CLUBS, AND GOLF CARTS

CHAPTER NINE

Tools for DamnfastDelivery

Chapter Nine
Tools for DamnfastDelivery

Speed is made possible by agreeing on a common process that will create a common language, common rules, common forms, and common reporting and communication channels.

To augment this common process, one efficient and effective tool that will quickly and accurately gather data on the driving issues under consideration are standardized formats. These guide individuals and groups in understanding the type of data required and the elements of the data that should be focused on. They provide a common way of describing and reporting massive amounts of information so it can be easily assimilated and compared for decision-making or action planning.

These tools can include:

- Integration Initiative Worksheet
- Executive Summary of Initiatives
- Project Communication Planner
- Retention Matrix

Sample Integration Initiative Worksheet

Purpose: Identify and prioritize the scope of current and combined work, overlaps, conflicts, gaps, and required support

Timing: Concurrent with business structure work and within two weeks of Strategy completion

Setting: Initial face-to-face followed by weekly conference calls

Level: Functional task forces

Core Initiatives	Start Date	End Date	Person Resp	Contribution to Results (Quantified)	Costs/ Hours (est)	Links to other Task Forces
1. Cross-sell (x-service/product) to Existing Customers 1.1 1.2 1.3						
2. Short Term Sales Infrastructure 2.1 2.2 2.3						
3. Establish Common vocabulary 3.1 3.2 3.3						
4. Build Sales resource model 4.1 4.2 4.3						

Sample Executive Summary for Initiatives

Purpose: Assimilate information from multiple task forces, ensure appropriate focus on issues, and measure progress against time requirements

Timing: Weekly following second week of task force work

Setting: Conference call

Level: Steering Committee

Initiative	Links to Other Task Forces	Open Questions Or Issues	Decisions Required	Resources Required
Cross Sell (x-product or service) into existing customers		What is the 100 day plan?		
Short term financial sales infrastructure		Are there any constraints on types of infrastructures to be considered?	Lay out short term sales geographies and responsibilities	Steering Committee
Build sales resource model		What are revenue expectations for next 8 quarters?	Expected revenue by quarters for next 8 quarters	Steering Committee
Define Marketing infrastructure		What is the planned IPO Date assuming revenue expectations are met?	Est. date for IPO	Steering Committee

Sample Communication Format

Purpose: A checklist to ensure all impacted parties have accurate information on merger events, expectations, progress, and their involvement; reduce rumors, anxiety, surprises; increase internal and external retention

Timing: End of first strategy session, weekly throughout project

Setting: Electronic and paper documents

Level: Created by task forces, approved by Steering Committee

Stakeholder(s)	Objective (Why?)	Message (What?)	Vehicle (How?)	How Often (When?)	Responsibility
Customers	Reduce uncertainty as to how this affects them, demonstrate their value through involvement	Excited about enhanced ability to serve, have a plan, broader range of products through one source	Visits with key customers by executives, direct letters and sales visits	Immediately on close, monthly on progress and process	
Suppliers	General announcement of merger	Pinpointed by future relationship priority		One time	
Board of Directors	Progress reports, no surprises	What, how, when of process and plans	Board meetings	Monthly	
Investors	Encourage them, let them know how you are enhancing their ROI	Synergies identified, work on schedule	Letter	Quarterly	

Media	Put positive spin on what is happening	Long term benefits in general terms	Phone call	At close	
Internal Organization	Reduce rumors, increase retention, encourageparticipation and support	Project structure, who is involved, what is expected	Group meetings, memos	Weekly	

Sample Retention Format

Purpose: Force explicit attention to key talent required to continue critical operations or intellectual capital, prevent
excessive expenditure on unnecessary stay packages

Timing: Immediately following strategy completion

Setting: Face-to-face

Level: Senior executives identify and interview

People/Groups	Impact of Loss	Motivators	Retention Action	Responsibility	Timing
S. Riddle	High	Direction & focus, being a part of the team and contributing	Decide on and announce his position in the new org.		1 week
M. Puzzle	High	Equity Position, Salary, Recognition for contributions, staff equity, inclusion in executive level discussions	50K additional stock, $10K additional salary, enlist him in the exec. Team		1 month
T. Scrabble	Medium	Having a direction to follow	None at this time		1 month
R. Monopoly	High	Challenge, Access to Execs, Contributing to org, equity position	Additional equity position that handcuffs him for 3-4 years (his words)		2-3 months

THE END

People We Would Like to Honor

To the invaluable members of the MergerCoach Family who have been with us from the beginning, and proved out the process in the field:

Ashley Ford Wiersma
Mark Gladstone
Kim Moriyama
Susan Buysse
Lindsay Geyer

To those special client project managers and friends, who have demonstrated the difference dedication, focus, and heart can make to their organizations during this process:

Sue Thompson, InFocus Corporation, Portland, Oregon
Terry Hamberger, Stonebridge Technologies, Atlanta, Georgia

To the First Readers of this book who gave it to us straight up:

GayAnn G. Smith
Peter Bottman
Jeri Epperson
Ella Cross-Miller
Dr. Steve Schepman

About the Authors

Susan K. Graaff—

Susan has a twenty five year track record of coaching executives in aggressively and effectively moving their businesses through tough decisions on strategy, structure and organizational design, system performance and cultural alignment. Since 1996 she has applied her expertise to the merger experience with great success. She partners closely with executives and staffs as they work to constructively align the power and politics of their organization, and to convert the energy of individuals into business results. Her experience spans diverse international and domestic industries. Susan authored "Mergers and Acquisitions from a Human Resource Perspective" in conjunction with Michigan State University's <u>Managing Human Resources in The 21<u>st</u> Century</u>, published by

Southwestern Press. She regularly lectures at three universities in the Pacific Northwest in graduate level courses on organization behavior and change management consulting. Her advanced degrees are in organization development and analysis.

C. Ray Rogers—
Ray held senior executive positions at Trane, Heil Quaker, and NW Bell Telephone before moving to an international consulting firm where he spent 20 years as Principal and Practice Leader in the U.S. and England . He has worked with diverse organizations that have a wide range of products and markets, in the United States, Canada, Europe, South America, and Asia. Ray's work with organizations undergoing significant change has been internationally recognized for its seminal thinking, innovation, and results. He is the author of a compelling first-hand account of the General Motors Cadillac Division move to autonomous work environments titled, <u>Transforming The Workplace</u>, published by Princeton Research Press. He also produced a five tape video lecture series on "Total Quality In Action", released by Communication Group Ltd.

0-595-26331-3

www.ingramcontent.com/pod-product-compliance
Lightning Source LLC
Chambersburg PA
CBHW030741180526
45163CB00003B/883